Ripley® Readers

All true and unbelievable!

Learning to read. Reading to learn!

LEVEL ONE Sounding It Out Preschool–Kindergarten
For kids who know their alphabet and are starting to sound out words.
learning sight words • beginning reading • sounding out words

LEVEL TWO Reading with Help Preschool–Grade 1
For kids who know sight words and are learning to sound out new words.
expanding vocabulary • building confidence • sounding out bigger words

LEVEL THREE Independent Reading Grades 1–3
For kids who are beginning to read on their own.
introducing paragraphs • challenging vocabulary • reading for comprehension

LEVEL FOUR Chapters Grades 2–4
For confident readers who enjoy a mixture of images and story.
reading for learning • more complex content • feeding curiosity

Ripley Readers Designed to help kids build their reading skills and confidence at any level, this program offers a variety of fun, entertaining, and unbelievable topics to interest even the most reluctant readers. With stories and information that will spark their curiosity, each book will motivate them to start and keep reading.

PUBLISHING

Vice President, Licensing & Publishing Amanda Joiner
Editorial Manager Carrie Bolin

Editor Jordie R. Orlando
Writer Korynn Wible-Freels
Designer Mark Voss
Reprographics Bob Prohaska

Published by Ripley Publishing 2020

10 9 8 7 6 5 4 3 2 1

Copyright © 2020 Ripley Publishing

ISBN: 978-1-60991-344-1

For more information regarding permission, contact:
VP Licensing & Publishing
Ripley Entertainment Inc.
7576 Kingspointe Parkway, Suite 188
Orlando, Florida 32819

Email: publishing@ripleys.com
www.ripleys.com/books
Manufactured in China in January 2020.

First Printing

Library of Congress Control Number: 2019954285

PUBLISHER'S NOTE
While every effort has been made to verify the accuracy of the entries in this book, the Publisher cannot be held responsible for any errors contained in the work. They would be glad to receive any information from readers.

PHOTO CREDITS
Cover © Vladimir Staykov/Shutterstock.com **3** © Vladimir Staykov/Shutterstock.com **4** © ESB Professional/Shutterstock.com **5** © Pixel-Shot/Shutterstock.com **6-7** © Africa Studio/Shutterstock.com **8-9** (dp) airportk9.org (Supplied by WENN.com) **9** (c) dpa picture alliance/Alamy Stock Photo **10-11** Paramount Group Anti-Poaching and K9 Academy/CATERS NEWS **12** © Monika Wisniewska/Shutterstock.com **13** © Kelly vanDellen/Shutterstock.com **14-15** (dp) © Ivonne Wierink/Shutterstock.com **15** (c) © home for heroes/Shutterstock.com **16-17** © Monkey Business Images/Shutterstock.com **18** © Rikshu/Shutterstock.com **19** © S1001/Shutterstock.com **20** © Marcel Jancovic/Shutterstock.com **21** © Leeloona/Shutterstock.com **22** Jose Luis Stephens/Alamy Stock Photo **23** © Africa Studio/Shutterstock.com **24** © Drazen Boskic PHOTO₀ Shutterstock.com **25** © alexei_tm/Shutterstock.com **26-27** (dp) © Christian Mueller/Shutterstock.com **27** (t) © Antonio Gravante/Shutterstock.com **28-29** © gillmar/Shutterstock.com **30** © Kzenon/Shutterstock.com **31** © mezzotint/Shutterstock.com **Master Graphics** © Vanessa Volk/Shutterstock.com; © bluebright/Shutterstock.com

Key: t = top, b = bottom, c = center, l = left, r = right, sp = single page, dp = double page, bkg = background

Ripley Readers

Dogs with Jobs

All true and unbelievable!

RIPLEY
PUBLISHING

a Jim Pattison Company

Dogs are more than man's best friend. They are man's best helper, too!

Many dogs have very
important jobs!

People who cannot see or hear may have helper dogs.

They can trust their pawed
pals to lead them safely!

Here is something to "bark" about... airport dogs keep birds off the runway when a plane is ready to take off!

Working dogs help animals, too, like the white rhino.

Believe it or not, some dogs jump from helicopters to chase rhino hunters!

Dogs are super sniffers! They look for dangerous things in bags, cars, and buildings.

Believe it or not, a dog's nose
is 50 times better than yours!

Thanks to their good noses, rescue dogs can find people after storms or accidents. No bones about it, they are true heroes!

Animals are so good
at making us smile!

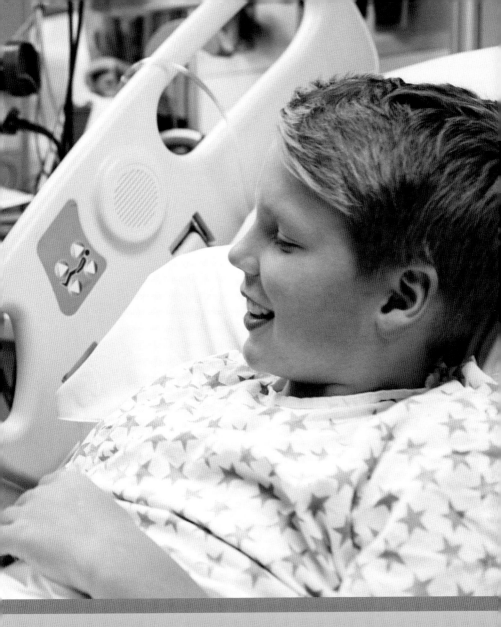

Therapy dogs bring joy to those who are sad, hurt, or sick.

Herding dogs work
hard around the farm.
They keep the sheep
safe and together!

Black-and-white collies are good at rounding up sheep!

This policeman is showing his shepherd how to catch a dangerous person.

You don't want to
mess with this pup!

Have you seen a dog open a door? How about pick something up?

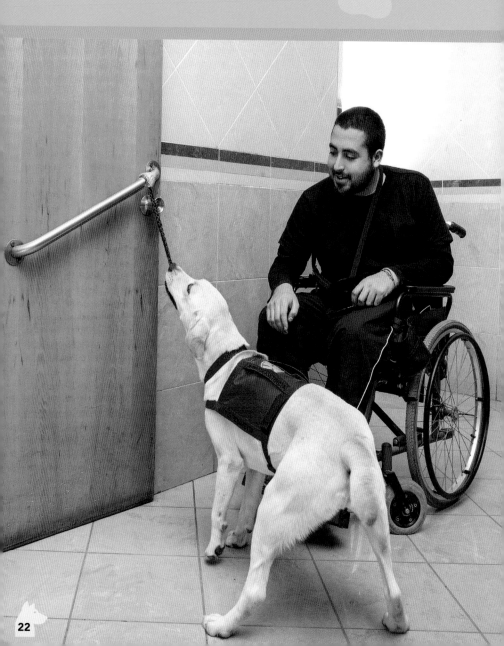

Dogs can be trained to help people in so many ways!

Does that dog look like it
is pointing? Yes, it does!

Hunting dogs show their owners where to look for birds!

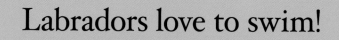

Labradors love to swim!

You can feel safe in the water
with these loveable lifeguards!

Have you ever taken
a ride on a dog sled?

Huskies can pull a sled for miles without stopping! They don't mind running in the cold.

You should always ask an owner before you pet a dog!

Maybe you would like to train a working dog one day!